# TERMINAL CANDOR

Donald C. Wilson

Foreword by
Paul R. Davidson, M.D.

Sutter House

Copyright © 1978 by Donald C. Wilson

*All Rights Reserved*


Designed and Published by
SUTTER HOUSE
Lititz, Pa. 17543

Cover design by
WILLIAM F. EARLY


**Library of Congress Cataloging in Publication Data**

Wilson, Donald C
    Terminal candor.

    1. Terminal care—Psychological aspects.
2. Terminal care—Moral and religious aspects.
3. Death—Psychological aspects. 4. Cancer—Psychological aspects. I. Title.
R726.W55      362.1      78-9911
ISBN 0-915010-23-2

PRINTED IN THE UNITED STATES OF AMERICA

TO BARBARA

I dedicate this testament of a sharing,

and

TO MY READERS

I commend the joy of discovering their
own mortality.

# Foreword

Death is the final event in the human experience. To some it comes unexpectedly and with great suddenness. Others are given warning of its approach and a time constriction placed on living. For all of us life is a strange admixture of success and failure, joy and disappointment, triumph and tragedy, ending in an aging process and finally death itself. We are ill-prepared for the realities of this. Why is this so?

Our country is by comparison with others very young, and our heterogeneous ethnic origins may play a part. The pressures that drive our production-consumption obsessed society glorify youth, materialism, self-indulgence, and have tended to vulgarize public tastes and values, and to undermine ethics and morality both public and private, as well as to dehumanize us in many ways. There is little time or energy left to develop cultural maturity and to deal with the basic needs of the human condition, particularly in the areas of tragedy and death.

Doctor Wilson has attempted to deal with these things from a background of personal experience with cancer. He brings to the task solid academic credentials, a life devoted to a very successful ministry in the Presbyterian Church, and a long experience in dealing with the problems of people. His intellectual integrity and ability to express his own deep feelings at this time offer us a rare opportunity for understanding. He has something to say to all of us, but especially to health and ministerial professionals. This book is a real contribution in a much neglected area of human knowledge.

Paul R. Davidson, M.D.

# Preface

These essays first appeared as a column in the Lancaster, Pennsylvania, *Intelligencer Journal,* from January to March, 1978. The encouraging response has suggested their wider usefulness in this collected form.

As a Christian pastor I was not insensitive to the characteristic impact with which a life-threatening disease challenges not just our "death awareness," but our whole pattern for living. Some of us react by trying to keep the "dying" and the "living" perspectives as far apart as possible. When my own cancer was diagnosed in January, 1975, what had been a pastoral point-of-view became a personal one. My wife and I had to work out — as individuals and as a couple — what our emotional posture would be. How much candor could we tolerate? Without ever actually sitting down to decide we found ourselves undertaking to bring the "dying" and the "living" together. In the ensuing months we have found we're not always successful. Fear and dread keep creeping in.

Nevertheless we wouldn't trade openness for the make-believe that is its only alternative. And the Holy Spirit who has nurtured Christians in bereavement through the centuries has confirmed His power in our experience to provide a "death that we can live with."

While the two essays on the Hospice movement are oriented toward the Lancaster County, Pennsylvania, situation, they are not merely of local concern. Indeed, the Hospice movement is the best symbol I know by which any community can measure it attitudes toward dying. For that reason I am including it here.

To new and old friends who have encouraged this compilation I extend my thanks, especially to Clair R. McCollough without whose support the project would have been impossible.

Donald C. Wilson

Pentecost 1978

# Contents

| | |
|---|---|
| The Great Obscenity | 7 |
| Should the Doctor "Tell"? | 8 |
| Denying One's Own Death | 9 |
| The "Other Shoe" Snydrome | 10 |
| Hoping | 12 |
| "The Pecking Order" | 13 |
| "Switching Baggage" | 15 |
| Explaining Death to Children | 16 |
| God and Our Pain | 18 |
| Praying to a Silent God | 20 |
| The Patient Looks at his Doctor | 21 |
| The Dying Patient and the Nurse | 24 |
| The Patient Looks at his Pastor | 26 |
| Walk, Don't Run | 27 |
| A Hospice Program for Lancaster? | 28 |

# The Great Obscenity

It used to be sex that was taboo in polite society, but no longer. Now it is cancer that is the great American obscenity. With all the medical miracles being performed, cancer is still a hold-out. Though certain forms seem to have yielded to therapy, we can't yet count on a sure-fire cancer cure.

Our trouble with cancer seems to stem, not just from its pathological stubbornness, but from the way it defies the standards we thought we lived by. We Americans have grown up on a rich diet of material expectations. From our birth we are programmed to succeed: "The difficult we do immediately; the impossible takes a little longer." Our technology, including our medical science, has conditioned us to great expectations. Indeed, it has given us the world's highest living standard, and I am not knocking that. The trouble is that cancer hasn't yet gotten the message that it is supposed to roll over and play dead, so we don't know what to do with it.

When my family and I first received my cancer verdict our immediate impulse was to seek out that specialist, that medical research center where they would have the cure. Of course there was a cure; the only problem was to find it. My local doctor had the sensitivity to recognize this inclination and arranged for us to have consultation elsewhere. But the possibility of limitation has a hard time taking root in all our positive thinking. In fact, it is almost unAmerican.

So cancer is not just a disease, as measles or tuberculosis used to be. It is the obscene reminder of our mortality. It is a potential way to death. And death, being a form of failure, is an embarrassment to our generation. It keeps reminding us that with all we can do, one thing we can't do is survive indefinitely.

Of course, there is nothing new in that, but our technological success has been bought with a price. A can-do culture has conspired with our human inclination to believe the good news and sweep the bad under the rug.

Nor has religion always been a help here. Sometimes religion has taken such a triumphalistic view of human nature that it has been blind to human failure, including the human necessity of death. When that has happened it has failed to help people endure the suffering that all living involves. It has held up unrealistic goals and actually diverted people from an awareness of God's presence when they are "walking through the valley of the shadow of death." On the other hand, a God who himself knows the experience of death can point a person toward one of life's greatest treasures — a death he or she can live with.

I don't pretend to understand how cancer, say cancer in a little child, fits into God's scheme of things. By all counts it is obscene. It offends not only American know-how, I believe it offends God even more. But one thing God can do: He can help us work toward a faith that will both give hope to the future and give meaning to the darkness along the way. If we will, as openly as we can, face the possibility of death, we may break down some of the isolating walls that a false sense of "failure" has put up. In fact, those who care most about us and would most like to reach through to us may right now be waiting for just such a signal.

# Should the Doctor "Tell"?

Should the doctor tell his patient that he or she has cancer? I believe that in most cases the prospective cancer victim "knows" already, and what he knows is the worst. In our day that is full of news of "wonder" cures and medical triumphs we are all so "cancer conscious" that CANCER is the first message that any unidentified symptom telegraphs to the brain.

The sudden appearance of blood in the urine or the lump in the breast spells, first and foremost, cancer. No doctor has to tell a person that. He got that far before he even picked up the phone. He suspected the worst. The one reaction more destructive than that is to be so paralyzed by fear as not to pick up the phone at all.

It is only after the tests come back negative and after the physician's thorough reassurance that one is persuaded he doesn't have cancer after all. I have a hard time believing that if the doctor does not mention the word his patient will never think of it. Rather, it is a case of being guilty until one is proved innocent.

Should the doctor "tell"? The question, instead, is how candid should the physician be with his findings? If the tests are negative, there is obviously no problem. But when the tests go the other way, the question then becomes, how honest should he be?

The columnist Stewart Alsop who went through terminal cancer put it this way for himself: "I want my doctor to tell me the truth and nothing but the truth, but not necessarily the whole truth." For one thing, it is obvious that the doctor does not have the whole truth. A terminal patient I know gets a macabre delight in telling how, four years ago, his doctor gave him three months to live.

But beyond the doctor's own fallibility, I am not sure I want the "whole truth" — at least not all at once. One needs room for hope. Not necessarily hope for a medical miracle, but a kind of spiritual and mental elbow-room in which to grow.

Browning said, "Grow old along with me; the best is yet to be." I only partly believe that. The best thing about growing old seems to me to be the opportunity to come to terms with the fact that I am going to die. To *know* that, through the aging process or through the onset of a terminal disease, may open one for the first time to some close encounters of a personal kind. That is why truth from the physician is so important.

Truth is the foundation for trust — all kinds of trust, trust in the doctor, trust in the future, trust among family members, trust in God, trust that today is worth living. When, for instance, the physician is able to talk honestly with his patient about his condition, where necessary acknowledging what he does not know, that openness can help open all kinds of other doors to deepening relationships between the patient and those about him or her.

So, from my doctor I want nothing but the truth. How much of the truth I get is partly up to me. For my doctor is going to read not just my biopsies, but also my emotional and religious readiness at the time. I suspect that, far more than we patients know, it is our signals to the doctor that tell him how much candor we are ready to bear. One cancer specialist with long years of experience says it this way: "I don't tell my patients; I let them tell me."

The trouble with this is that it leaves out the physician's own attitude toward death, for his patient's death confronts the doctor with the reminder of his own. It also represents for him the defeat of his efforts as a healer. I, as a patient, have as great a stake in his ability to come to terms with death as his similar expectation of me. So I appreciate the physician's sensitivity when he says he lets his patients tell him. But if both of us give in to our human reluctance to face the distasteful, the result is distrust and fence-building at a time when they are least needed. Candor, like charity, begins at home.

## Denying One's Own Death

*Q. I have been reading that denying one's own death is the worst thing to do. But is it any better to just lie down and give up?*

A. Right on. I couldn't agree more. On learning, for instance, of some life-threatening onslaught, it is by one's denial that he or she stakes out his claim to survival and plans the counter-attack. Denial sets up the command-post for the ensuing combat. I think of that U.S. officer in World War II who, when confronted with the Nazis' command to surrender, replied, "Nuts!"

Moreover, even Dr. Elizabeth Kübler-Ross whose book, *On Death and Dying*, has become a classic on the subject and who documents denial as the first of the "five stages" of anticipatory grief, acknowledges the looseness of the pattern. I recall fondly a parishioner of mine who was a spinster with a stalwart faith and not a relative in the world. After learning that her case was terminal she never did advance from denial, to anger, to bargaining, to depression, to acceptance. She went to her death still denying.

As helpful as this idea of the stages of grief is, there needs to be a lot more research done before it is seen as more than theoretical.* Meanwhile those of us who are trying to come to terms with our own death and be helpful to others need to avoid badgering the other through the stages of an ideal pattern. While faith in God's power and eternity can be a genuine help, the person who has spent a lifetime denying its vexations is apt to respond similarly to death's.

Notwithstanding the tenacity of that impulse to deny and its positive role in self-preservation, we need to be aware when we are practicing it. Denial, like the Devil, has as its chief strategy persuading us that it does not exist. I think of the husband and wife who were having a heart-to-heart talk about death when the man suddenly stated, "If one of us dies, I'll go to Paris!" But to deny death can, as it were, be fatal. Carried through unacknowledged to the end, the denial of impending death can have tragic consequences. It can shut out dear ones, it can frustrate openness to God; it can prevent therapy that might have made a

---
*See Daniel Leviton, "Death Education," in Herman Feifel (ed.), *New Meanings of Death*, New York: McGraw-Hill, 1966, p. 260.

difference. I know of no better illustration of that subtle balance between denial as evasion and denial as a strategy of survival than the words of a middle-aged man dying of melanoma: "I know I'm dying but I don't really believe I'm dying."*

This is really the flip side of the statement made to Jesus, "Lord, I believe: help my unbelief." With that kind of selfawareness God can do something. Denial of our mortality is pretty deeply ingrained in us, but we don't need to compound the problem by self-deception. The supportive resources of the Christian faith and the Jewish faith, as I understand it, are lost to one who is unprepared to acknowledge his need.

I know how easy it is to fool myself. As I look back I have found some dandy ways. First, I have told myself, "Sure, you are going to die, but not for a long time yet." Then in my work as pastor I visited dying persons and said to myself, "You are not where they are. They are dying but you are living." Finally, I deny death right now by treating it as an academic subject, writing about it for the newspaper. Sending in the article I banish the subject. Out of sight, out of mind. I'll bet some of you are just as talented in the art as I am.

When, in addition, we are surrounded by others who encourage the self-deception it is hard not to persist in the unconscious denial. Physicians who are denial-prone can retreat from their patients behind some life-sustaining machine. And ministers with unresolved death anxieties can cover over the subject and shut people up with, "Let us pray." I'm not belittling the place of prayer: we'll have more on that later. But unless prayer springs from where the patient is, rather than where the clergyman wishes he were, it will probably become another wall between the patient and those who need to share the experience with him. The greatest of God's gifts to us is our faith. I don't think God wants us to use it against truth and against that part of living that we call dying.

Yes, denial of death is part of our affirmation of life, but denial becomes destructive when we imagine we are fooling ourselves.

## ⇛ The "Other Shoe" Syndrome ⇚

There is a condition shared by many — probably most — cancer patients. I call it the "other shoe" syndrome. The diagnosis was made and treatment begun some weeks or even years ago. That was when the "first shoe" hit the floor. Now, if the patient is not actually in remission, the new symptoms present themselves infrequently enough to be almost taken in stride. One is coping with the vexations of the disease and its treatment.

One finds himself nearly believing that there may be a way out. Yet all the while the senses are poised, waiting for the "other shoe" to fall, the time when once again the sentence is pronounced.

Parents who have had a child in and out of remission have been through the

*Laurens P. White, "Death and the Physician," in Feifel, op. cit., p. 100.

process again and again. And they ask themselves how much a person can endure. In fact, it seems to me that those who stand by have a harder time riding the roller-coaster than the patient.

It is more accurate, I believe, to speak of "fatal" illness than "terminal" disease. Strictly speaking, the fatal illness becomes "terminal" at that time when the symptoms defy further treatment. The medical people have no more rabbits to pull out of the hat. When this truth is acknowledged by doctor, patient, and family, it may be said to be the beginning of the terminal period. Though one may not yet have arrived at that stage, the prospect of doing so after a series of lost battles does contribute to the anxiety of the "other shoe" syndrome.

Well then, what to do about it? I can think of no better answer for myself — or for any person, sick or well — than to follow the title of Orville Kelly's program: *Make Today Count*. This remarkable newspaper man, finding himself with cancer, resolved not to give in to the disease or surrender to the psychic desolation. Yesterday is behind us and its benedictions can be acknowledged. Tomorrow is a chapter yet to be written. But today is where we are with the materials that are at hand.

What a telling testimony to making today count we saw in the latter months of the life of Hubert Humphrey! Self-pity, withdrawal, bitterness — I am sure all of these were options considered and rejected by the Happy Warrior. For him they would have been out of character.

For dying is a part of living. To be waiting for the "other shoe" is not the unique experience of the cancer or heart victim. As that eminent commentator on the contemporary, Archie Bunker, observed, "Everybody's gotta die sometime. That's life." All of us are waiting. For each "there is a time to be born and a time to die." To have a life-threatening disease is merely to "have been put on notice." I suppose to one in good health it does seem morbid to contemplate his own mortality. But having been put on notice can put a zing in living.

For one thing, all my life as a pastor I have been preaching the promises of the resurrection in Christ and the power of his atoning death. Up to now I have been distributing faith's checks. Now I am starting to cash them for myself — to find out if they are negotiable in the market-place of today. No special warning ought to have been necessary to make me appreciate the value of the moment. I have been privileged to share the dying and bereavement experiences with others. They have taught me more about dying and living than I can ever repay.

But, given the nature of the beast (The Apostle Paul calls death the "last enemy"), for me, cancer has given a fresh urgency to today. Being put on notice has brought a new sense of the support of my family, a broader awareness of the mutual dependence of all of us under the shadow of mortality, and finally a confirming audit of the Gospel of Christ in the here-and-now. Jesus knew how to shed yesterday's load, to travel light, and move into the unknown.

Admittedly, this is the finding of one individual with his own particular make-up, his own tradition. Many of you who are also "under notice" have discovered your unique ways of living today to the fullest.

# Hoping

*Q. My mother, age 54, has been a convinced Christian since my early childhood. Now she is in remission with leukemia that was diagnosed 19 months ago. I find it strange that at this stage of her life she does not make greater reference to the power of prayer and her expectations for eternal life, and give a more active witness to her faith.*

A. Perhaps she is not yet ready to — and for an understandable reason. While the power of Christ and the promises of the resurrection may be basic to her faith in God it is possible that at present other hopes are dominant in her understanding of reality.

I believe that God expects even the Christian to be true to his own apprehension of his life situation. Because your Mother is not trying to "witness" to her family does not necessarily mean she is denying the faith. Indeed, I find my attitude akin to your Mother's. Each of us has to be true to where we are, not to where even our family thinks we ought to be.

What we hope for at any one time depends on many factors. Certainly one is our perception of our situation. A patient whose condition he and his doctors have acknowledged to be terminal will have one set of hope aims. These are determined by the fact that he or she is already in the *process* of dying. (I take it your Mother does not so perceive herself.) Under these circumstances a person may be entertaining extravagantly false hopes — bargaining ("God, if you will send me a miracle cure, I will spend more time with my family.") Or, as that terminal patient moves closer toward death, the prospect of relief from pain and, depending on religious tradition, the hope of everlasting life will probably move to the forefront of his or her hope agenda.

On the other hand, those for whom death is not yet a present *process,* but still only a future *prospect* may be entertaining a different hope agenda. As one who is in the latter category I can report how my own array of hopes has undergone transformation. When my cancer was first diagnosed, I confess that the hope for everlasting life was not my prime concern. Survivial was. I hoped, and was encouraged to hope, that a cure would be found. To be sure, those two hopes are not mutually exclusive. One can hope both to survive and to continue living beyond death at the same time. It is a matter of predominance.

Then I found as time went on and I was not pronounced cured, that some more limited hopes took over. The closing of one avenue can mean the opening of others. The hope for a medical cure remains but others arose as adjustment to the new life situation became apparent. I hoped, and hope, to "make today count." I dare to hope that I will be able to find meaning in the present experience, even to be of help to others who are walking the same road. It is here that the supposedly dormant Christian affirmations in your Mother may be making themselves felt in unseen ways. This is just a guess, but may it not be that the "power of the cross" is helping her to an understanding of what is happening to her; or that the "power of the resurrection" may be generating new beginnings in the personhood of herself and those around her?

Other hopes that come before a person at a time like this may be just the hope for more time. I know I would like to see my four-year-old grandson get into adolescence. Also, it wasn't until reaching this stage that I gave much thought to my own dying: I hope I will die a "good death". I haven't spent much time on this hope, but there it is, and it has started to bob around in my consciousness.

So much for the ways that one's hope agenda can change between the original diagnosis and the onset of terminality. Is it possible that your Mother also may be somewhere along this road?

When and if it comes to the terminal stage one who is not yet there can only surmise what his hopes will be. For one thing, I see no reason why my hope aims will not continue to evolve. At that time, those that have been only dimly perceived will probably take on a new urgency: hopes for one's family in their adjustment to the loss, hopes for their financial security, hopes that one's life's work will not go down the drain – a kind of immortality through influence. Then too, I suspect, there will be a greater stake in a "good death" – that the pain will be manageable, that one will retain his faculties as well as some measure of dignity.

The experience of others suggests that in the normal course as death approaches, the patient (as well as those surrounding him) begins to prepare for the separation by "distancing," a leave-taking from those whom he has loved. As I imagine myself at that place I hope (now) that those bonds that have given life its meaning will hold fast through the physical detachment, to be resumed when we shall all be re-issued, as Ben Franklin put it: *In a new and more elegant edition, revised and corrected by the Author.* This, at least for now, is what I hope I will hope.

In any event, I suspect that in our dying as in our living, what we hope for is a rather sure guide to where we see ourselves. I hope that my hoping will be true to reality – not a form of denial or evasion. When dishonesty is that close to home it is hard for those who love us to reach through to an authentic person.

## "The Pecking Order"

"I can recall the hour in which I lost my immortality, in which I tried on my shroud for the first time and saw how it became me," wrote the American writer, Ben Hecht, in 1954. "The knowledge of my dying came to me when my mother died...I accepted death for both of us."

Apparently the mere fact that we are born human does not guarantee that we naturally arrive at the full realization of our mortality. In the lives of some of us this dawning of awareness represents a kind of new death and new birth. "Perhaps a person does not become fully adult until death has been recognized as an authentic companion to life."* Whatever else "maturity" means, it seems to indicate that one has worked out a relationship to both death and life, not just in one's mind, but down in the emotions as well.

We have spoken before of our technological age demanding specific answers, requiring predictable performances. All the while, mystery and uncertainty — the unpredictables — are part of the human experience. And death doesn't let us forget them.

Mr. Hecht's experience is characteristic of our age in that his awakening did not occur for him until midlife. In primitive cultures the "farewell to innocence" was often linked with the puberty rites of passage. With these folk death-awareness came earlier. With us our first bereavement frequently does not come until, with children of our own, we face the death of a parent. The fact that people are now living longer is a relatively new occurrence. We've almost forgotten that through most of human history death was mainly the scourge of children and of women at child-birth. When we say of a young person's death, "He was too young to die," we are reflecting an event that used to be commonplace. This shift in the time of dying has brought significant changes in attitudes.

What happens when a middle-aged person loses a parent? Generally, our society is ill-at-ease with showings of grief. What there is should be over and done with. This is especially true when death has occurred to one "whose time had come." But for the middle-aged person who mourns this is the first close encounter, and it's relatively late in the game.

In Ecclesiastes the Preacher tells that there is "a time to be born and a time to die...a time to mourn and a time to dance." He is putting his finger on a defense mechanism that has meaning in any generation. Robert Kastenbaum calls it "the pecking-order of death." Most of us use this in one way or another in making our private arrangement with death. Under its auspices we are led either to accept our dying or deny it.

While we may not consciously work it out this way, the assurance that there is "a time to die" leads to the expectation that the oldest of those we care about will die first. This is as it "ought" to be. That those who die will do so "on schedule" has two important consequences.

First, it is a source of comfort. While we may feel a bit guilty about acknowledging it, the fact that there is a certain logic in Death's approach shows that at least it is "playing by the rules". As long as there is a "time to die" I can rest assured that my number will not be coming up for a while. This is the good news—

—But then the bad. The logic of the pecking-order brings its own dread: Though death is still at arm's length, it does keep getting closer. When my own father died when I was 27, my grief was essentially at the loss of a father. When my mother died 24 years later there came a new realization: I was next in line. So a death whose timeliness may bring a certain reassurance to the survivor may also reduce the distance between that person and his or her own "time."

Sometimes this certainty is too oppressive to think about and we rev up our will to banish it by deliberate denial. If we come out of a religious background

---

*Robert Kastenbaum, "Death and Development Through the Life Span." in Feifel, op. cit., p. 19.

we may be tempted to do this by a "pious pole-vault". That is, we tell ourselves that the remainder of our life with its anticipated troubles, including death itself, is of little count compared with the joys of heaven. So, rather than using faith's resources to give meaning to life's heartaches, we use them to pole-vault into a premature refuge in the life after death.

The Apostle Paul found himself tempted by this very option of going to "be with Christ." But on reflection he decided that, rather than putting all his eggs in the heavenly basket, God still had work for him here (Phil. 1:21-26). One of the challenges of midlife is replacing that old what-is-becoming-of-me with a new who-I-am-still-becoming. It seems to me to be the difference between a brittle defense and a springy offense. The rebirth at middle-age may be a preview of the commmencement that Easter certifies for the Christian death.

## "Switching Baggage"

Most persons facing a life-threatening disease would like to think of themselves as having the courage to face alone what lies ahead. Somehow it seems almost cowardly to let others in on our troubles. Hell should be endured privately. We'd rather be caught dead than parade our self-pity before others.

The only problem with enduring privately is that life-threatening disease doesn't strike privately. When an individual is afflicted, his family and friends are automatically involved. Oh, he or she alone bears the disease, but each of them bears a related load. You can't love a person and not hurt when he or she hurts. A spouse will wonder: Will I be able to cope with the patient's increasing helplessness? Possible disfigurement? Then there are mundane matters like money. Will there be enough to see us through? How about afterwards? The fears of resuming an unknown future alone?

So each family member (and friends, to a corresponding extent) finds himself carrying an unexpected load. In fact, the total burden of grief is actually greater than the sum of its parts. For when anxiety and pain are carried privately, there is the added weight of loneliness.

True, there is no substitute for bravery but if it ignores the burden that another is also carrying, it can be a form of selfishness. I am thinking, for instance, of the cardiac patient who after his second heart attack said to me, "My wife has troubles enough of her own. She doesn't need me to load my fears on her." The consequence of this "quiet endurance" often serves to increase the anxiety level for all.

With all the reminders of our helplessness, there is one thing we can do to help carry the load. That is, pass it around. The Apostle Paul counseled his friends to "Bear one another's burdens and so fulfill the law of Christ." (Gal. 6:2) This amazing insight into human nature is really the essence of our belonging to one another. Paul was suggesting that what I can't do for myself, another can do for me; what the other can't do, I can do for him. The women in the

Scilly Isles off the coast of England illustrate this truth by doing one another's laundry!

A life-threatening illness has a unique capacity to depress us with our helplessness and frustration. One burden we don't need to add is the sense of being alone. Another is resentment of the self-inflicted burden of "keeping it to ourselves."

Suppose I suddenly discover that down the road I have to travel, I am now required to carry a 200 lb. suitcase that I hadn't planned on. That is more that I can lift. Then I find at the same time that those around me also have to carry correspondingly impossible loads — different colors and shapes, to be sure, but equally unmanageable for them. As we tug in helpless frustration, we are approached by the Guide who has gone this way before. At his word each of us looks across to the other's predicament and reaches over to lift the others baggage. And the impossible happens. What I can't carry for myself can be carried by another. What keeps it from being a cop-out for the courageous person who dreads being a "free-loader" is that each one has his hands full — with someone else's load.

To be willing to chance that kind of a baggage shift calls for trust and sensitivity and a special kind of courage. That combination the Guide sometimes called "love."

## ⇛Explaining Death to Children⇚

*Q. What suggestions do you have for a person learning her life is to be cut short—regarding the mental and emotional adjustments, particularly for her children?—J.L.*

A. Child psychologists tell us that at least as early as age two, children have some conception of death. Since the possibility of their own death or that of a loved one is an ever-present reality with children, you are being both wise and considerate in facing the subject with them. In the games they play, the stories they hear, the TV programs they watch, children are constantly dealing with death. Yet most American parents are more open about sex with their children than they are about death. They face the question, "Where did I come from?", but they duck the question, "Where am I going?" Several studies among bereaved children give substantial evidence that those who have discussed death before a parent died fared better than those who had not.

So, painful as it is for you to raise the question concerning your children, the very fact that you are doing it may not only be of help to them, but will involve your own preparation as well. Where to start?

Have the children had a pet die? I'm not equating the death of a pet with the death of a loved one, but any death encounter brings an opportunity to try on, rehearse, so to speak, some of the feelings that come when death moves closer in. Should I have taken better care of my pet? Will it come back? Where did it go? Can I get a new one? Is it all right to cry? When these kinds of questions are allowed to surface, the parent has some idea of what the child is thinking. Moreover, it provides a precedent for discussing the prospect of one's own death.

Before some observations about interpreting death to children, here are some Don'ts. Don't tell children fantasies that even you do not believe. If Heaven is real to you, fine. But don't invent it for the children's sake. The Christian concept of everlasting life is too real a support to be counterfeited. Don't camouflage death by describing it as a trip or sleep. Both of these come to an end, and both can become objects of fear. Don't tell children God wants good people. Though it may be true, it can raise more problems than a child (or even an adult) can handle.

It has been my experience that all of us need to share memories and feelings with one another about life's important events, including the death of someone close. This is especially true of children, and parents, church, and school have marvelous opportunities. To avoid opening the subject for fear of making a mistake will in itself be communicating the wrong message to the child. Should death take on the aura for a child of such overwhelming catastrophe that strong adults cannot even talk about it, then the child may be on his way to deepseated problems about the future in general.

In opening the subject with your children here are some things to bear in mind: First, when a loved one dies, children may in some sense hold themselves responsible. With the "magical powers" that children possess, they frequently wish someone dead. When it occurs, it's not hard to imagine their feelings. Remember that children look for reasons. They ask the "why" questions and frequently blame themselves. They will supply a "cause" whether adults discuss it with them or not. So, careful explanation of how and why the person died can be the best way of dealing with childhood guilt.

Second, behind all the child's apprehensions about death is the reality of separation. What is really bothering children is their fear of being deserted. The assurance that they will not be abandoned or left alone needs to be stated and reinforced. It is here, too, that the affirmations of one's faith can support those human bonds that tie us together in this life and the bonds of faith in the life to come. If the child sees human bonds holding through the strains of daily living in this life, it will come to trust them for the future.

Finally, there is no substitute for creating the environment in which children express their feelings and their thoughts. Children's feelings about the death of a loved one are the same as adults'; they may just express them differently. An illustration of the way certain brothers and sisters reacted to terminally ill children was given by Dr. Myra Bluebond-Langner of Rutgers University.* She tells of how mothers became disturbed when siblings responded to news of a brother's or sister's death with such expressions as, "Good, now I can have all his toys". Later the mothers came to understand that this was the way children express such feelings as anger for being left alone (a feeling shared by parents) or

*Myra Bluebond-Langner, "Meanings of Death of Children," in Feifel, op. cit., p. 63.

of holding on to a part of the deceased (a desire of parents, too). In preparing children for a death in the family, the children themselves may afford the best cues. They have many ideas right and wrong. If they are encouraged to ventilate, we can deal honestly with today's questions today. Tomorrow they will be back, but farther down the road.

And letting our children know we are open may lead us adults to our own deepening awareness.

## ⋙⋙⋙⋙⋙ God and Our Pain ⋘⋘⋘⋘⋘

*Q. Dear Sir: I was in the same lost condition you are in for 57 years of my life and know the agonies of mind you suffer. Can't you just look to the risen Christ and say the sinners prayer? I will be praying for you. — W.G.*

A. I am thankful for your prayers. It is reassuring to hear from you and others that I am not praying alone. By the "sinner's prayer" I take it you are referring to Luke 18:10 ff.:

> *The tax collector beat his breast, saying "God, be merciful to me a sinner!" "I tell you," said Jesus, "this man went down to his house justified."*

My problem is not about God justifying sinners such as myself. The "agonies" to which I assume you are referring have to do rather with the bewilderment at human suffering in the plan of a loving God. What is comforting is that these very agonies were experienced by the apostles and our Lord himself.

Let's look at two of them—pain and separation. First, at one time or another, most patients of a fatal illness have asked, Why is this happening to me? The Apostle Paul found himself with some kind of physical affliction that he never clearly identified.

> *A thorn was given me in the flesh, a messenger of Satan, to harass me. (II Cor. 12:7)*

In other words, it hurt like the devil! And Paul didn't take it lying down.

> *Three times I besought the Lord about this, that it should leave me. (II Cor. 12:8)*

Apparently it never did, but in the experience Paul came to an amazing insight: The affliction turned him inside out, specifically it opened the door to God's presence. Through enduring the pain and sharing the burden of it with his fellow-believers Christ became more real to him, and his sense of who he was as a person came into sharper focus.

Why should it work out this way? Why is it that more often in suffering than in joy, on rough water than on smooth, a person's true being comes through? In Paul's case, the answer apparently was that his real identity came in dependence on Christ. He was most a man, not when directing things, but when he was on the receiving end. "I am content with weaknesses...for when I am weak, then I am strong." (vs. 10)

Certainly this is not all the answer to why we humans have to endure hardships like illness (why don't we require a similar "answer" to the problem of joy?), but at least there is one meaning to it. To be mortal means to be dependent— on God and on one another. We are never more human than when we acknowledge that this is so.

Secondly, greater than the distress at not finding meaning in our suffering is the fear of abandonment in facing death. Many parents and children give vent to this dread every night at bedtime:

> *Now I lay me down to sleep.*
> *I pray the Lord my soul to keep.*
> *If I should die before I wake,*
> *I pray the Lord my soul to take.*

This is another way of expressing, however unconsciously, what we stated above, that we really only exist to the extent that we are tied to God.

Obviously, the dread of non-being is heightened at those times when death draws near. With Jesus Christ it was no exception: 'My God, my God, why hast thou forsaken me?" That prayer gasped toward God from the cross was in itself a claim to relationship. Though the words expressed God's felt withdrawal, the cry was a link between Son and Father. And it has tied hurting men and women to God ever since. I can think of no more authentic symbol of God's openness with humankind than that cry of Jesus.

When a person confronts a fearful event such as a personal disgrace, a fatal disease, the death of a loved one, it is typical for that reality to have an isolating effect. One stands singled out, cut off, abandoned. Whatever promises of reassurance may then be given us gain credibility if they come from one who, like Christ, knows what it's like to himself have felt abandoned.

Funeral sermons often make the "pious pole-vault" from life to eternal life, and the dying that comes in between gets lost. But what was happening to the deceased while he or she was still living and having to go through the dying? Was he allowed to give vent to the feelings about the forthcoming separation? Was there opportunity to say goodbye?

Or was the agony so painful to the patient or the family it had to be denied? Everyone acting as if the patient were going to live? The charade may relieve the witnesses but it can build walls around the patient. One woman said to me, "My family doesn't even talk to me. A minister came by and he could only talk about salvation. It's as if I'm already dead."

Because Christ made our agonies his own they are the very reason that faith becomes a living option for the one who faces his dying.

# Praying to a Silent God

In one form or another the question keeps recurring: How long is the Christian with a life-threatening illness justified in going on praying for a healing miracle?

Jesus promised, "Whatever you ask in my name I will do it." (Jn. 14:13) And he told the story of the widow who, taking her pleas to the judge, refused to take no for an answer. By sheer persistence she badgered the judge into granting her petition. (Lk. 18:1f.) Jesus told his followers to pray like that. Even to pray for healing?

Paul must have thought so. We've earlier referred to his prayers for relief from his "thorn in the flesh" (II Cor. 12:7f.) "Three times I besought the Lord about this, that it should leave me." Paul must have had that promise of the Lord in mind when he did this. In addition, the past evidence of God's power in his own conversion must have encouraged him to ask. But evidently the Lord had other plans and told him, "My grace is sufficient for you." (II Cor. 12:9)

Well, like Paul, I have done my share of praying for relief — and more than three times. How long does one go on trying to pry a miracle from a silent God? I have concluded that, on Jesus' own authority, one is never to stop praying for that. In addition certain other possibilities suggest themselves.

1. There is still no substitute for dependence on God. His power, Paul found, can best be seen in our asking. The widow's persistence, Jesus' promise, his own faithfulness through Gethsemane and the cross, all testify to that. Ask, ask, ask. God wants us to "take it to the Lord in prayer."

2. God's love for me and for those I love is greater than my own. Hence, hard as it is to accept, he is more aware of what is good for us than we ourselves. In the parable of the widow and the judge, Jesus was pointing to the widow's persistence, not the judge's likeness to our heavenly Father. Though God welcomes our requests, as a parent welcomes his child's dependence, God doesn't need to be instructed about what is best for us. He knows better than we. Indeed, the basis of our dependence is "thy will be done."

3. Thus, the answers God gives in the events that mark our journey through life are one way of his teaching us what to pray for. I believe he answers all our prayers. What we assume to be refusals may be his attempt to have us change the direction of our asking. To pray "in Jesus name" is to do our asking more and more in that conformity to the mind of Christ that life's experiences have taught us. God's "silence" in the face of Paul's request for healing suggested that God — while still loving him — had other plans. Even the pain and vexation were to be pressed into that service. Indeed, death itself was to be part of living.

4. We have spoken before of the changing focus of prayer. Our hopes can change and prayer changes accordingly. Since death is going to come to all in one form or another, why such a big deal if I suspect that for me it will be through cancer? Perhaps God wants me to spend less time trying to avoid it and more time giving meaning and even joy to the time remaining. Thus, to be with-

out immediate expectation of a physical cure is by no means to be without hope. Paul speaks elsewhere of "hoping against hope." (One of my modest hopes has come to be the giving of some support to others who are taking a fresh look at their own mortality.)

We have no word from Paul that he stopped praying about his "thorn in the flesh" after the third time, but I am sure that he was heartened by word from his friends that they were going on praying in his behalf. But for a person to keep playing only the stuck record is to miss the other new tunes that our Lord intends us to dance to.

5. Finally, if the promises of the risen Christ mean anything, they hold out that the life beyond this living is full of a love and a beauty of which we have here only a dim reflection. Certainly, the human wish for survival would make me welcome the chance to prolong the present bonds of human love. Nevertheless, I suspect that when we find ourselves exploring the fresh scenery of that "house of many rooms" we will wonder to ourselves, "Why did it take so long?"

Meanwhile, standing at this remove from those precincts, there remains a lot to pray for: faith, hope, love. Thanks for the fresh evidences of *faith* that affliction has opened up. Asking for wider vistas of *hope* beyond a physical reprieve. Intercession for God's *love* wherever one person is helping bear another's burden.

# The Patient Looks at His Doctor

When I first took my as-yet undiagnosed cancer to my doctor I was laying a time-bomb in his lap. Now looking back on that encounter I know I have put an agonizingly demanding task before him. As I come to the realization of the probable course of this illness I find myself wanting two people from the one physician. I want a technical professional. That is, I want the best medical help available. Second, I want a human professional, that is, one who will deal with me not as a disease but as a human.

Until recently that was an aspect of medicine that medical schools didn't spend much time on. But with cancer's reminder to medicine that it still has a long way to go, the human aspects of patient care loom large. When *curing* is beyond the physician's reach, *caring* moves to the front burner. It would seem then, that medicine is as much an art as it is a science.

From where I sit somewhere between the initial diagnosis and whatever the end may be, my respect for the medical profession is enhanced by what I have seen in the doctors with whom I have had to do. That experience has led me to some high expectations of the physician not just as a medical but also as a human professional. Specifically, from my doctor I want five things.

1. I want my doctor to be in touch with his own or her own feelings. Before he can be aware of what I am going through, he needs to be aware of his own experience, particularly, his experience of failure. For if my case is fatal, it does

mark a defeat for all that he has been trained to do. He has defined his vocation as a healer, and as Dr. S. E. Adelman writes, cancer "defeats my whole picture of the world, in which I am all-powerful, defying disease, knowing more than the layman, initiate into the secrets of disease, immune to old fears and superstitions."* His tools, his education, his support system, most important, his own expectations, have equipped him for success. The dying patient confronts him with guilt and with a painful reminder of his own mortality. If the patient is "brave" the doctor may be able to suppress his emotions. But when anxiety breaks through the patient's defenses, then his demands on the physician's own involvement increase. I don't expect my doctor to welcome failure, but I do need him to face it — and to go on with me from there.

2. I want my doctor to be in touch with my feelings. When, for instance, he is explaining the diagnosis I am apt to hear only what I am prepared to hear. As the doctor is tempted to deny, so is the patient. The psyche has a way of censoring its own intake. My doctor needs to know that he may have to go over the same ground at a later time. Parents recognize how selective children can be in listening to instructions: "I didn't hear you tell me to clean the garage!" So my doctors needs to know where I am when he is telling me.

In a deeper sense I want my doctor to be aware of my feelings. If there is anyone who has a greater stake in my case than the doctor, it is I. I want my doctor to recognize my role in our relationship. To the extent that my physician enables me to mobilize all the resources of body, mind, and faith he is performing the highest arts of the healing profession. Norman Cousins in *The Saturday Review* (2/18/78) quotes Dr. Gerald Looney of the Medical College of the University of Southern California: "Nothing is more out of date than the notion that doctors can't learn from their patients...I teach my students to listen very carefully to their patients...That's what good medical practice is all about." I suspect that as the course of the disease progresses and the patient's ability to function independently becomes more and more restricted, it will become correspondingly essential for the patient to have a say in making decisions about those choices still open.

3. I want my doctor to be honest. By this I mean I want to be told the facts and in detail. I want my diagnosis by name; I want to know what my prospects are; I want the details of the treatment, the side-effects of the therapy and the physicial limitations that are foreseen. The doctor may tell me too much; he may not tell me enough. What I can't stand from him is a lie.

Candor is the basis of our relationship and it has to last the course. The patient who, following the initial diagnosis and treatment, has a recurrence, presents the doctor with an even more complex psychological problem. When this happens, writes Dr. Benjamin F. Rush Jr. of the New Jersey Medical School, "the surgeon tumbles from his high place."** Well, the know-how for a cure

---

*Quoted in Jeane Quint Benoliel, "Anticipatory Grief in Physicians and Nurses," in Bernard Schoenberg et al. (eds.), *Anticipatory Grief,* New York: Columbia University Press, 1974, p. 221.

**Benjamin F. Rush, Jr., "A Surgical Oncologist's Observations", in Schoenberg, op. cit., p. 103.

may be out of human reach but the integrity of the patient/doctor relationship becomes all the more important. If trust has been absent before, it will be hard to generate it now. On the other hand, trust that has been built from the start may be one of the most potent resources during the terminal period.

4. I want my doctor to involve my family in the treatment. They are already involved in the illness. If I know one thing about my condition and my family knows another, our communication is diminished. When there is discouraging news I am not sure that I will be alert to cover all the bases. Here the physician must keep control. One professor of medicine, Laurens P. White of California, puts it this explicity: "I make it a point to try not to discuss diagnosis and prognosis with the family without the patient being present. In this way everybody knows at the same time what everybody else knows, but, more importantly, everybody knows that everybody knows, and that different stories are not being given to different people."*

But the doctor's role as a human professional goes beyond conveying the relevant information. When the doctor lets the patient and family know that he is including the family in his care, that assurance gives encouragement to each of them in their own respective roles. A family group can be compared to a mobile hanging from the ceiling. Every move by one member prompts a corresponding movement of every other member and the whole family. Other health-care professionals can play a part in harmonizing these movements — nurse, pastor, social-worker. But for the physician as executive director of the caring ministry there is no substitute.

5. I want my doctor with me to the end. Let me tell you a secret. When I ask my doctor how long it will be to the end I am not necessarily asking for a calendar date. What I am really concerned with is whether the physician will be with me all the way. I can think of no more heartening answer than: "I don't know how long you are going to live, but I'll tell you this — that however long it takes and whatever it takes, we will go through it together."

I expect to need him as a fellow-human after he has outlived his capacity as a technician. If he sees that his usefulness to me is ended when he has no new treatment to prescribe, he is not only deserting me but he is denying the value of his own humanity.

A five-year-old boy suspected he wasn't going to get well and asked his doctor. The doctor told him he was very sick and the treatment had not been effective. He asked the boy if he was afraid. The boy asked the doctor if he was afraid. They both decided they were not. When the boy told his parents that everything would be all right, they asked him how he knew. "Because my doctor loves me," was the reply.

The Apostle Paul told us that "love is patient and kind." Impending death that prompts the doctor to wonder where he failed prompts the patient to wonder if he is worth it. The patience and kindness then forthcoming from the doctor can mark the difference between prolonging living and prolonging dying. It ought to be the right of each of us to live until we die.

*Laurens P. White, op. cit., p. 99.

# The Dying Patient and the Nurse

Except for the dramatic image of Florence Nightingale, most of us have given little thought to the role of the nurse among care-giving professionals. This lack of public recognition undoubtedly reflects the relatively low social value that we attach to those occupations traditionally defined as female. But when it comes to the lonely passage of dying there is no more significant professional presence than that of the nurse. Indeed, a perception of the vital role of the nurse would certainly not have come home to me had it not been for my own experience and impending need.

Consider, for instance, the nursing care of the dying: If the physician bears the brunt of the sense of the loss of power represented by a patient's death, the nurse too is not immune to the frustration. As with the physician, and in common with all humans, the death of a patient confronts the nurse with his or her (odds are it's "her") own mortality. And few of us go out of our way to meet death. In a recent meeting with 17 R.N.'s and L.P.N.'s I found only three who said they preferred assignment to terminal cases. Let's look a little deeper at some of the reasons why this may be so.

For one thing, since those days of the "lady with the lamp," the traditional means of giving personal care to the patient have been intercepted by the increased use of medical technology. As in many other fields, the machine has crowded out personal contact, and the more's the pity for both giver and receiver. The sense of personal reward that comes with giving a sponge bath to bring down a fever is not the same as the satisfaction in giving a pencillin injection.

When it comes to nursing the dying patient, there bristles a whole nest of special problems that are not found with the recovering. The nurse is under particular stress when her patient's pain is difficult to manage, or if the dying is prolonged, or when she finds that the imminent death is going to break emotional ties that have formed between her and the patient or family. Add to these the stress wherein she is required to continue "heroic measures" indefinitely beyond possibility of recovery. Or most difficult of all, if the true prognosis is being withheld from the patient, the nurse is in an emotionally and profesionally untenable position. What those nurses I mentioned above were objecting to was that they were having to play a deceptive charade. No wonder terminal care is not an odds-on favorite with nurses! Yet the nurses are expected to stay on the case and control the whole atmosphere of the surroundings in which the patient's life draws to its close. As one of the nation's most respected teachers of nurses, Dr. Jeanne Quint Benoliel puts it: "Far more than is true for physicians, nurses are in positions to influence the social milieu of dying and to set priorities based on the patient's stated wishes."*

So as I look forward to my need of nursing attention, each specific requirement will depend on that professional having, in addition to technical compe-

---
*Jeanne Quint Benoliel, "Nurses and the Human Experience of Dying." in Feifel, op. cit., p. 134.

tence, a desire and capacity to work with me as a person. From nurses who have helped me in previous hospitalizations, I have learned a personal respect for this form of ministry. Christ himself lifted up the care of the sick when he said, "Inasmuch as ye have done it unto the least of these...ye have done it unto me." Specifically, I see four ways in which the terminal-care nurse can fulfill this calling.

First, since the terminal stage will represent a massive change in all areas of my life-style, my nurse can be the prime mover in normalizing the living pattern under its altered conditions. We have spoken before of the patient's sense of failure and damaged self-worth that comes with the awareness of impending death. Compared with the majority of other patients in a general hospital setting, the terminal patient does not consider himself one of the "star boarders." Within the limits of the doctor's orders and my own preferences, whatever my nurse can do to make the place of dying to be as a place of living would be in the highest tradition of her art.

Second, she can make the most of whatever opportunities there may be for me to share in the decisions that need to be made. I have needed nurses already and know how dependent a patient is. But dying may be said to begin when the dependence is no longer optional but obligatory. Thus, *social* death may begin long before physical death and it is in that climate that she can by thoughtful concern involve the dependent one in imaginative questions that keep him in touch with his reality.

Third, of all members of the health-care team, nurses are in the position for opening communications between the patient and his family and others about him. True, if my doctor or family should decide that my true prognosis is to be withheld from me, my nurse's task is increased immeasurably. But assuming there is no mandated roadblock, it is her opportunity to foster and encourage the patient in "tidying up" his unfinished business, in creating the climate for her patient to say goodbye to people – and even hello to God.

Finally, my nurse can help me find what may be called an "appropriate death," that is, the kind of death a person would choose for himself if he had a choice. Right now as I write these lines and as you read them, we are both on this search for a death that we can live with. At terminality the search begins in earnest. My nurse has the opportunity after heroic intervention has been left behind to help me and my family pack my bags and allow death to come as a friend in the context of open and quiet waiting. The nurse's professional demeanor and her own readiness to accept can enable the patient to die while he is still alive.

# The Patient Looks at His Pastor

It is the Christian story that the way through the loneliness of pain and death is by way of the broken body of Jesus. In fact, loneliness is around us from the very beginning. Not even the minister is immune to it. Indeed, the profession of being a clergy-man or -woman signals its own brand of loneliness.

Here is one who has an urgent desire to give meaning to people's lives but an industrial and technological age doesn't have much time for what he has to say. He doesn't seem to be among those invited in where the decisions are made. Add to these the competitiveness that shows through on the newspaper's religious pages, and the wounds of his own isolation can sink deep into the one who is called to bind up the wounds of others.

Yet to the extent that the pastor is willing to face his loneliness, he is in the singular position to help me when my time comes to face the isolation of dying. Anger at my particular misfortune, resentment of the healthy, shame at my failure, guilt at omissions and commissions of a lifetime — all these, in spite of myself, build walls that increase loneliness. So what I will need from that one who has been called the "wounded healer" is the assurance that he is in this mortality with me. In fact, without his wounds — however sincere his intentions — the minister is useless. As with Christ, so with his servants: His hurt is the badge of his authority.

Specifically, what I won't want from my minister, then, is a rosy picture of the heavenly bliss. If he takes the pious pole-vault over the unpleasantness of my dying into the sweet bye-and-bye, then he is like the man Harry Truman described as unable to stand the heat of the kitchen.

On the other hand, the validity of my pastor's call to my bedside will be certified in several ways. As Jesus contemplated his own death in Gethsemane, he asked his sleeping friends, "Could ye not watch with me one hour?" I will want a presence, first of all, that without necessarily saying anything affirms "the silence of eternity interpreted by love." Being a clergyperson myself, I understand the demanding task of being at the bedside, not because one ought to be there but because one wants to be. It is a sign of our isolation that, as a rule, ministers make poor parishioners and never more so than when they are patients. But if he is there because of his calling and not because of his obligation, the healing will have begun.

Second, by sharing my pain there will be fresh hope. When I can become aware that I don't have to evade what lies ahead, but that others are sharing that with me, then the pains themselves can be changed from signs of despair to signs of hope. The minister won't be the only one sharing. It should certainly involve the family, but often the family who is unused to this kind of openness can be helped by the pastor. I know of one such pastor who by thoughtful listening at the bedside encouraged a dying wife to confess her fears for the future of her children to her husband. Not till then was the husband able to express his own doubts about being able to cope without her. After the wife's death, it was the memory of this sharing that helped him most in his bereavement. By switching burdens — doubts, guilts, rage — the unbearable burden is carried. And the pastor who knows these first-hand in the climate of God's healing and forgiveness can show the way.

Finally, the pastor can lead in the rituals of our leave-taking. This is especially his function. I put it last because that is where it must come in the sequence of credibility. The rituals surrounding death are those traditional ways of acting that enable the wounded to pick their way through the uncharted thickets of emotional trauma. These call for the pastor's sensitive leadership. All of these assume a reality and power in the context of a hurt that is shared. The pastor represents the community of faith and that community is now closing ranks around its hurting members. Outside this context the liturgies of our faith become not only artificial caricatures, but they embarrass and alienate. Within, they point to that One who, standing watch and ward over our broken hopes "has borne our griefs and carried our sorrows."

## Walk, Don't Run

A funny thing I've discovered — people are dying to talk about death. Letters and comments from so many of you indicate a desire to end the conspiracy of silence surrounding the anxieties we all share about our dying. Indeed, this was what prompted my own search and these writings.

As I come to the end of this writing, I find myself with a consensus and a conviction. The consensus is that of all the subjects we have discussed that one drawing the most interest has had to do with the prospect of a Hospice for Lancaster County. It would seem that the idea of an open approach to dying, which Hospice represents, gives us the opportunity to bring our fears and hopes about our dying into a manageable focus. That our death or that of dear ones might come out of the closet and that it could take place in surroundings of both comfort and communication somehow brings our dying into the scope of living.

Thus, a Hospice represents not just a place for the terminally ill but, quite apart from any individual's need to go there, it stands as an entire community's fresh approach to dying. I see, in short, a consensus growing toward that end. That consensus needs discussion by all of us — physicians, nurses, hospital and nursing home administrators, clergy, social workers, lawyers, and all who are willing to acknowledge our one common bond — mortality.

Narrowing the range from consensus I come down to a very personal conviction. It is that facing our dying improves the quality of our living. The Psalmist ended his 23rd Song with the assurance that he would "dwell in the house of the Lord forever." For the Christian that will mean, of course, coming into the fullness of God's grace in the life everlasting.

But apart from the glory of death, I am finding that there are some real rewards in facing death before it takes place. That same Psalmist stated that he "walked through the valley of the shadow of death." That is where some of us are finding ourselves right now — in the valley. Life appears a matter of months, not years, not decades. When the fact of our dying first comes homes to us, our reaction is often to take to our heels and either run pell-mell for the light at the end of the tunnel or try to slither past the harsh realities by ignoring them. Not so the Psalmist. He is willing to "walk" through them, taste them, if you will, as another aspect of the mystery of life. I take it this is something of what Jesus meant when he told us to "take up the cross" and follow him. My conviction is that we can neutralize the "sting" of death by facing it. So the valley of the shadow of our dying is to be experienced at a walk, not a run.

Then if we are moving through it at that pace our eyes have time to get used to the darkness. In that darkness we may be able to detect what we have not noticed before — that there are others with us in the same shadow. They too are lonely, grieving, frightened and as much in the need of our hand as we are in need of theirs. If, on the other hand, the prospect of our dying panics us into a run, I suspect it will be pretty much every man for himself and the devil take the one who's last.

But when we are moving at a walk, hand can reach out and touch hand, fears can be shared, burdens can be lifted. Like the Psalmist we may find that, never more so than in the valley of dying, we are in the presence of God.

# A Hospice Program for Lancaster?

## Pro

Does Lancaster County need a Hospice? The Hospice movement was begun in 1948 by Dr. Cicely Saunders at St. Christopher's Hospice, Sydenham, England. The movement identifies itself as furnishing a caring program solely for the terminally ill. They operate in the understanding that the dying patient can be most humanly treated to the extent that that person, together with family, doctors, nurses, clergy — all — openly face the fact of the patient's impending death. The Hospice movement has already had considerable influence in this country on the care of those in the last stages of a fatal illness. A separate Hospice facility may or may not be part of the Hospice program. The heart of the program is the nature of medical/nursing/family care whether administered in a Hospice or in the patient's home.

After the curing resources have been exhausted, those who are ministering to the dying have not forfeited their human, comforting and emotionally sustaining ties with the patient. Though the patient may be past *curing*, those around him or her are not past *caring*. In the openness of this caring context the person dying in a Hospice program is led to a fresh awareness of that aspect that is still unique to being human — personal integrity.

Hospices are obviously special hospitals. Their kind of cure marks them as a "movement" whose philosophy applies outside their own walls, to home-care, nursing homes, or general hospitals. The physical pain associated with particular forms of dying is considered an illness in itself, to be diagnosed and treated with attention to detail. Pain is treated in light of the whole range of the patient's distress — emotional and social — as well as physical. Eighty percent of the patients at St. Christopher's have pain sufficient to need narcotics for its adequate relief. "Drugs balanced to need and given regularly so that pain does not occur prevent the vicious spiral of pain, tension, increased pain, and a higher dose of analgesic," says Dr. Saunders. "The best treatment of terminal pain is its prevention."

Does Lancaster County need a Hospice unit? Or is the care of the dying finding adequate expression in our present health care facilities? This is obviously a technical question whose answer must come from those in the several professional disciplines involved. What are my credentials for raising the question? Two: First, thirty years as a pastor ministering to individuals and families in the death experience. Second, that vested interest that comes with facing the prospect myself.

Below, then, are some of the benefits of a Hospice program to our community as they appear to one, admittedly, not disinterested observer.

*1. Openness toward death.* When all who are involved acknowledge to themselves and one another death's nearness, then honesty is not just a matter of policy, but is the climate for the final confrontation. As a father said of the Hospice after his daughter's death, "She knew that they would never tell her a lie. When you are dying, this can be more important than any medical treatment."

*2. Patient integrity.* One of the most important contributors to patient care is the patient himself. Interests, desires for participation, room decor, personal idiosyncracies, when taken into account, convey the sense that the dying one is maintaining some control over his own dying. There is little sense of hurry — that feeling that someone more important, more seriously ill, demands the nurses' attention. The incoming patient who has been a "failure" in the acute ward and to his physician often feels obscurely that it is his own fault. Terminal care should continue to affirm the patient's own sense of personhood.

*3. Family involvement.* When a patient desires to have a member of the family present until the end, another bed may be wheeled into the room. Wrote one daughter after her father's death, "I came to know my father better during those days and nights we had together. To be aware of death without being afraid of it seems to make one that much more aware of life."

*4. Pain control.* So far from patients "having to earn their morphine," as a British physician explained the practice at his general hospital, narcotics are so administered as to maintain the pain at a minimum level. One result is an actually smaller intake than when given only on patient demand. In the latter case, the temptation is almost overpowering for the patient to be so "brave" as to go past the point where relief can be achieved by minimum dosage.

5. *Teaching.* The existence of the Hospice movement has already contributed to terminal care practices in other institutions. As Hospices become more prevalent so will their influence in areas where they may not be feasible. Such a facility, modeled after St. Christopher's, is already operating in New Haven, Connecticut.

## ⋙ Con ⋘

It should be evident to those reading *Terminal Candor* that I would be hard put to find a single reason against the concept of an open approach to dying by family and health-care professionals. In that sense there can be no "con" or negative argument regarding the patient approach of the Hospice movement.

Notwithstanding, there are some debatable aspects to establishing a separate facility to provide care for the terminally ill. Let me name a few:

*1. Beyond healing?* Similar to the question, when is a person medically certified as dead? is the question, when is a patient medically certified as "terminal" (that is, beyond the possibility of healing)? Since the general hospital contains the full resources of therapeutic care plus the capacity for analgesic control (that is, both the operating room and the pain pill), to be pronounced "terminal" and transferred to a Hospice program is to leave behind the instruments of diagnostic and curative care. Is medical diagnosis exact enough in specific cases to determine that the patient has passed the point where no more healing should be attempted, and hence "isolated" from therapy.

*2. Financial limitations.* There would appear to be at least two:

a—The first applies in case the Hospice program has determined there is, indeed, need for a separate Hospice facility. With medical costs soaring and present bed occupancy below capacity, it is not justifiable to siphon off potential funds to establish a separate physical facility for the limited number of terminally ill.

b—Where present health-care costs are being financed by insurance and/or Medicare programs, their purpose is the restoration of the patient to health. The Hospice, then, though supplying skilled medical care, might find itself outside the range of eligibility for this kind of funding, and therefore beyond the reach of ordinary families. (One factor bearing on both the above financial considerations is that per-bed costs in a Hospice should be appreciably lower than in a regular hospital where patient fees are needed to bear the cost of a multitude of different services, such as diagnostic equipment, laboratories, operating rooms, with their attendant personnel.)

*3. Standards for admission.* What qualifications would be set up and how fair would they be for selecting patients for admission? One can foresee that the setting for an "appropriate death" could become a luxury within the reach only of those who could either pay the bill or be the privileged patients of certain physicians. With a single program of this type, its entrance qualifications would have to be as open as those of our hospitals.

*4. Drug limitation.* It is my understanding that several of the kinds of drugs used in England that play an integral part in pain control are legally unavailable for physicians' use in this country. Unless the law is changed or adequate substitutes are found, the effectiveness of any Hospice program would be severely compromised.

*5. Symbol of reproach?* If the advocating of a Hospice program for our community were interpreted as evidence that our present hospitals and nursing homes were not doing their job, obviously the plan would fail and would deserve to fail. The Hospice movement is not a judgment on present medical, hospital, or nursing care. In these respects our county is singularly fortunate. However, like intensive care or physical therapy, the Hospice is another specialty — providing a setting for the "appropriate death" for the terminally ill. But because of the chances for misunderstanding here by those who are most directly responsible for making it work, there is no point in pretending that the Hospice movement may not seem to be a symbol of reproach.

Whether there is any significant dialogue in our community over the possibility of establishing the program, it is my hope that addressing ourselves to the pros and cons may encourage the broadest consideration of what it means to have a "good" or an "appropriate death." The subject is of concern to a wider audience than either the professionals and volunteers who would make it work or potential patients who might be future candidates for a Hospice bed.